WHAT SHOULD WE ALL DO
AFTER THE
TRAYVON MARTIN TRIAL?

Thank you for your support enjoy the read!

Terrence R. McCrea

Terrence R. McCrea

Copyright © 2015 by Terrence R. McCrea
Long Beach, California
All rights reserved
Printed and Bound in the United States of America

McCrea's Publishing Company
Long Beach, California
Email: terrence5580@sbcglobal.net

Packaging/Consulting
Professional Publishing House
1425 W. Manchester Ave. Ste B
Los Angeles, California 90047
323-750-3592
Email: professionalpublishinghouse@yahoo.com
www.Professionalpublishinghouse.com

Cover design: TWA Solutions.com
First Printing: December 2015
978-0-692-58195-7
Library of Congress Control Number: 2015920603
10987654321.

DEDICATION

This book is dedicated to my mother, Leslie Jones. I thank you for all the encouragement you have given me. You are truly the wind beneath my wings.

ACKNOWLEDGMENTS

To Dr. Maxine Thompson, I thank you for helping to bring out the very best in my writing skills. You made me think deeper within my thoughts and I will forever hold on to what you taught me about research when writing.

To Dr. Rosie Milligan, Thank you for assisting me in publishing my literary work. Thank you for seeing my literary potentials. I appreciate the help that you have given the many new writers, and thank you for hosting the Black Writers On Tour Conference.

INTRODUCTION

On Feb 5, 1995, Trayvon Martin was born in Sanford, Florida. Three weeks after his seventeenth birthday, on February 26, 2012, as an unarmed teenager, he was shot and killed by a 28-year-old man who was on a quest to kill. This 28-year-old predator profiled and made an arrogant decision, based on his own ignorance, as he closed in on his prey. America basically told us that we are not allowed to walk home while being cold, black and alert.

February 26, 2012, the life of this black male was taken by a so-called helpless non-black who allegedly couldn't defend himself against this "angry black male." After this black male lost his life, it took police 46 days to make an arrest on the non-black killer who unlawfully profiled a human being.

Then, as if to add insult to injury, on June 24, 2013, this horrific trial caused us to become emotionally drained as we sat and watched America profile the black race once again. On July 13, 2013, Black America was killed spiritually and mentally by the two words, "Not guilty."

These words will forever haunt the hearts and inner beings of young black males as they try to navigate through this discriminatory treatment between authorities and young black males.

How has it come to this? As you may well know, America's popular culture influences the perception of non-Black Americans, who are corrupted by the continuation of Black stereotypes. These stereotypes are sometimes suggested or triggered by the news analysts, as well as the social media. Once Americans put their thoughts and opinions on the Internet, people on opposing sides will surely have a rebuttal.

In the movie, *Menace II Society*, Charles S. Dutton's character says, "Being a black man in America isn't easy.... The hunt is on and you're the prey."

This seems to be exactly what happened to Trayvon Martin. He was hunted, tracked down like an animal, and then killed.

Everyone wants to judge young Black males based on the way they look and the way they act around certain people. Some are not aware that most of us are misunderstood inner-city kids who sometimes have no idea what our future will hold. There are some people that mock our character, based on the color of our skin. They judge us because we don't apply ourselves according to their standards of American society.

Many people see us as ignorant and uneducated. Although it doesn't matter how others see us when it comes to education, more importantly, it depends on how we carry ourselves as young Black men. Education is so critical to our self-esteem, yet we become threatened by people with higher positions than us because we assume we can only dream of achieving their accomplishments. These people don't understand our lifestyles because America perceives us to be drug dealers, killers, and thieves.

This problem is further compounded by the poverty in the inner cities, which cause us to separate ourselves from one another based on the Crip and Blood gang wars that non Black Americans find entertaining. Unfortunately, the rap music and black images in popular culture cause non-blacks to perceive most of us as what they may hear in the lyrics or see on the screen.

If one were to argue more black men are being killed by the hands of white policeman, some non-blacks would quickly point out the fact we kill each other. A person who would make such a statement will often think the life of a black male is meaningless and unworthy of living, as if death by a gunman is a favor. They never mention white-on-white crime, but 90% of white murders are done by other whites because that's who lives in proximity to them. The same issue with Black-on-Black crime. People tend to kill people who live in their surroundings.

Back to the Trayvon Martin verdict, as protesters awaited the verdict outside the court building, the young people from both sides of the case were in a frenzy as they waited to get their thoughts and opinions heard. Will the American people actually comprehend what we have to say or is everything just a conspiracy? America's popular culture makes black people appear as savages, thieves and killers. These are misconceptions that cause us to separate ourselves from each other as black people and as Americans.

Since slavery ended, America has caused some blacks to believe what they want us to believe as they discuss and debate about their personal experiences. Some non-blacks seem to judge us based on the color of our skin, instead of the content of our character. Some Americans are unaware that black images in popular culture are used to perpetuate the stereotypes from slavery. Some public figures are even brainwashing the minds of young black Americans. As the media present "bling bling," which many urban youth feel they can't afford, it creates a longing for luxuries that are not necessities in the hearts of youth. Needless to say, this materialistic society has a tremendous effect on the crime rate in black communities.

Although sometimes Black youth project these stereotypes upon ourselves, we have no choice when we are pushed away because of the mistreatment we face in society.

As human beings, we are judged based on our skin color. We are left with uncertainty through most of our lives. Time seems to be moving faster as we go on in life, yet we never find our own purpose. Once we all get back in touch with reality, some of us lack the necessary resources within our communities that will help us appreciate what America has to offer.

"Not guilty" (Jury's voice). "Not guilty!?" (Our incredulous voices). Not guilty are the two words that have left black communities all around the country at an emotional stand still. Black Americans are stuck with two questions. What are we to do next? And how far have we evolved as a country, both non-black and Black America? Most of us assumed that America would think with their hearts or minds and not their racial ignorance, but as time went along, racism continues to become a major factor. The post racial society that we are supposedly living in with the first African American president is a fallacy.

Why? Because as a society, we have not evolved that far since black males are still being profiled and killed. Law enforcement has used the excuse of drugs and intoxication to back up their reason for pulling the trigger on black males. I think it's safe to say that I can speak for young and older black males when I say that we were not really surprised at the Trayvon Martin verdict, but we did think justice would be served because we thought this country had moved on from their ignorant state of minds.

Following the trial, there were several probing questions for which Black and non-black people still want answers. The entire trial was a travesty of justice. Further, America mocks the ignorance of Black Americans around this country through popular culture and social media in order to perpetuate their stereotypic point of views. America does not care about the war between black males and law enforcement because no matter how educated we become or what we may contribute to society, we will always appear as "niggers" to non-black America.

We could take time to protest all we want, but will the rich racist whites with power and authority stop and listen to the race they have held in captivity and confinement? These are the prejudices that have continued to pile up against the black race since slavery times. It seems as if non-blacks look at all of us the same way no matter what we do.

There are some genuine non-blacks that give everyone the benefit of the doubt; however, the majority misinterpret the trials and tribulations that black males face every day within our communities. A close-minded American is quick to debate their truth behind their lies. They come up with a liable explanation to verify it. Although we are entitled to our own opinion, it seems when the black male has one, it's wrong or inconclusive.

In society, some of these people grow up misunderstood and without the self-respect they need in order to be at peace with themselves. American society has young black Americans so confused that we are angry with ourselves, our family, and especially racist non-blacks.

CHAPTER ONE

What Can We Take From This Indignant Verdict?

As we sit and wait to see if civil rights charges will be presented against George Zimmerman, we are left skeptical on whether any charges will even be filed. Allow me to be the first to say, we must wait no longer. Black people, it's time to pull ourselves together and emerge as one. Both blacks and non-blacks were disheartened by this outrageous verdict. Many Americans were thrown out of their chairs when they heard those shocking two words, "Not guilty."

As of October 18, 2013, there are still people who want the legal procedures explained in a more logical manner. This case cannot, and will not, ever be swallowed by black Americans. It will never be accepted by any of us. I challenge White America. Do not use this fuel for a revolution; use this case as fuel for development of your character's inner-being.

There are enough blacks that have been killed and incarcerated. It is time for us, as Blacks, to live as open-minded people, to free ourselves from the mental frustration. We should maintain our purpose without limits or low expectations. Let us no longer sit back and wait for the world to change for us; let's go out in the world, put forth our best efforts, and see how the results end.

If we, as a people, don't get ourselves together, then we will never have the power that we all desperately need to thrive in this country. We all should be on our own mission, which will build roads to success as we live on with society and help the people in it. We shouldn't give into other people's negative opinions so that we can figure out our own directions as we move on. We all have those times when we doubt ourselves, usually based on what other people say about something we want to do. In time that can cause us to look past our true historical backgrounds where we, as African Americans, made significant contributions to this country.

Even if we are considered blacks or "niggers", why shouldn't we become more educated? If some black kid from the inner city of Chicago can become president, then who's to say that a black kid from Los Angeles can't become a lawyer or a black kid from New York can't become a doctor? In other words, we need to understand that it's not always based on where you're from, but mainly where you're going.

The moment this verdict was announced, America was expecting a dramatic outcry from black communities all across the country. They were expecting blacks to be the violent beast they presume the majority of us are and, in some areas around the country, we gave it to them. The police, along with other authorities, can be so predictable in our communities. Surely, if you have ever encountered the experience of harassment with them, you can truly see the enjoyment in their facial expressions, body language, as well as their stance. This black victim was doing nothing, just as we are usually doing when we are stopped by police. In this instance, however, the killer was not a cop; he was a simple-minded individual who wanted to be Spiderman.

At times, some black people question their unknown feared capabilities. We always put off recurring important themes of discrimination and police brutality, as if we are scared to face them in reality. Sadly, at times we are. As we live on and we are on a mission to beat the system, we never give it up for as long as we live. It is mandatory that we take the time to discover our other side so we can play all sides together.

From the time slavery ended, we have been at the bottom of almost every statistical category. There is not one significant thing that we are at the top of, at least when it comes to education. We have the media to give us a blow-by-blow description of how racist our society is. As you look at the factors of the case, you can see Americans still have racism in their hearts.

The positions they put Trayvon Martin in were hindering for his side of the argument. George Zimmerman's argument did nothing but become stronger when compared to the civil rights of the 17-year-old victim. When we heard "not guilty," our hearts dropped to our stomachs as we thought America would show this dead teenager some respect. Since the victim, (along with his church-going parents,) had enough respect for himself to fight back to try and save his life, he still didn't get any love from this country. For most young people, this was the first nationally televised trial that we watched all the way through. All we could do was sit there and watch them spit in our faces. We watched our dreams get shattered right before our eyes as we heard the two dreadful words, "Not guilty." Everything we thought we could be seemed to disappear after this trial because it killed our confidence. We thought America would sacrifice their racial ignorance this one time just so young black men and women could feel justice was served.

We must take advantage of this frustration and use it as fuel to move forward with personal purpose.

CHAPTER TWO

B ack in slavery days, it was against the law for us to read or be educated, and many, such as Frederick Douglass, struggled to read so they could be free. Yet, unfortunately, many young people, unlike our ancestors, still live on as if we don't care to learn to read. We young blacks fantasize about the thug life we see in popular culture as if that lifestyle is a way to make it out. We don't focus on what we can actually do in reality. If we see an educated black male that we call a square, we mock and ridicule them, as if they are meaningless to our community. Sometimes, educated black men are called "white washed" in our communities. The ones who call someone of their own ethnicity "white washed" usually don't know what black means. People who call someone else "white washed" based on their educational background must be an ignorant person themselves.

Is this illusion true or is it the people that are not becoming educated that would be considered white washed? White washed would have to mean falling in the hands of white people and making their presumptions true. The only way a black person with wealth can be white washed is if they are bird-minded thinkers. As an inner city child, you see the differences of a person's mind based on the way they treat you. At times, our environments determine how far we can go in life at times and no one seems to understand that. We engage ourselves in activities that make us look like typical "Niggers" to the racist white man. As we socialize with our peers, we get caught up in our "Tall Tales" conversation and we forget about reality. When we socialize we judge each other based on the similarity of our lifestyles. As we see our peers engage in illegal activity, we start to follow behind them and become another criminal statistic. The thug mentality runs through the bone. If we live on this mentality, it will run through us for the rest of our lives. It's hard to get rid of. As we are caught up in our own personal thug mentality, we don't respect anyone else's. When living this lifestyle, the only outcome can be death or life sentence in prison. There are millions of us who think the thug life is all we need to continue in our lifetime. Even if we are sure it won't help us, we will always think and feel it is the way to live in this country. In front of our peers, we shy away from emotional feelings in order to make ourselves look "hard." Not being able to say how we feel to someone can damage our personality. The overwhelming peer pressure is put on us by our own young people, and sometimes by our older family members if they are "OGs." We are sometimes forced into these gangs or associations. Since we can all relate to each other when it comes to our unrighteous experiences, it agitates me to a certain extent in the sense that we seem to worship the one-sided thought that it's okay to not have feelings, at least according to the thug life. We steadily maintain this cocky ignorance, falling right into the white man's hands. I don't recall any stereotypes about us having an education, but there are several that implicate us as not having an education and not having an interest in seeking one either. I assume that since we have slowly started to progress individually, we have already moved past these judgments of educated black men and we can now stop overlooking them. One thing we should start with is respecting ourselves because it's one of the reasons why we can't respect others. Once we learn how to respect ourselves, we can learn how to respect our community and our peers, both black and non-black. Even though there has been a slight improvement, it seems as if the black race has done nothing but become more impaired over the years. In terms of business ownership, economic power and political control, we have seen very little progress. This verdict brought out intense emotions in all of us who have empathy for human life. However, do not respond with negativity towards the system. Start by getting yourselves together so we won't have to live in low- income housing areas. Positively challenge yourself to fight the system with hard work and dedication. It's time for us to live life on a mission to establish ourselves for the future and for our future children. In this case, if something similar to this happens again in our legal system, we will be prepared next time and ready to protest even more in order to seek justice. As impossible as it seems to make that change, it's very important that we at least speculate on it.

When we do, it becomes certain that we will also have our future generations ready for this critical American country. Black men and women, if we procrastinate on our elapsed self-esteem, we will continue to perpetuate the constant cycle that we witness some of our parents struggling through today. As an inner-city citizen, I have to demolish the delusions of grandeur, such as viewing gang membership as prosperous and necessary for our evolvement. The true lifestyle behind gang membership is gruesome. This does nothing but destroys black families and keeps our communities unprosperous. To people outside our communities, this causes them to judge our character in a negative way. Non-blacks that see this generation's behavior in the media speculate and believe these stereotypes of us collectively. There are times when we think about our decisions and we find relief from our negative reality in order to come back to our own closed world. We run from the truth so we continue to engage in environmental mishaps. All of us know there is nothing that comes out of being a part of a gang. Some of us don't even have to be from any gang affiliation, but we could just be from the struggle of the streets. As soon as someone outside our community comes in to cause trouble with us, we are furious because they are disturbing the peace. As a black person, life is very hard when you have to play both sides against the middle in order to keep your cool with certain people. Many of us are all victims of black-on-black crime. We all have lost family behind it, but why haven't we stopped to think about what we are truly doing to each other? Along with everything else that the Black community faces, such as white supremacy, colorism, and self-hatred we have for ourselves, black-on-black crime does nothing more than undermine our progress . It also causes emotional setbacks for black families.   Clearly, we realize that killing one another hurts us all in the exact same ways, yet we still turn away from this reality. If we can generally relate to each other from the standpoint of our similarities, no matter the financial background, we could flourish as a population.

CHAPTER THREE

As abysmally unjust as the legal system is, in the Trayvon Martin case, they sent the court of public opinion on an emotional roller coaster for sixteen hours, only to result in a "not guilty" verdict based on one seemingly debatable law. Considering the fact the killer conducted himself with so much irresponsibility, it's a sure fact that Trayvon Martin had his rights violated more so than the adult who should have had more sense and wisdom than the seventeen-year-old victim. Once again, racist white America passed up another opportunity to properly analyze our black lives. Clearly, this case wasn't about the victim; it was about the aggressive suspect.

George Zimmerman supporters are not humane individuals. Obviously, they didn't care for anyone else's life, except the non-black that stayed alive. It's indigestible because the supporters of George Zimmerman are overlooking the death of a young teenager. Beast or no beast, Trayvon Martin is still equal to all of us as humanitarians.

America, let's make this clear. If that were a twenty-nine-year-old black man killing a seventeen-year-old white male, there is no question he would have at least received a sentence of manslaughter. I mean, let's be realistic here. In this case, you would infer from the start, and you would assume the jury would have found some sneaky law that would have revoked the "stand your ground" law. If they focused more on the dead black child, it should have taken less than sixteen hours to debate and discuss a way to get the killer behind bars. George Zimmerman was the focal point of the entire case, and the six racist jurors spent sixteen hours trying to find a way for the killer to be set free.

CHAPTER FOUR

Why is it Important for us to Learn our History?

Black history is the history of all Americans when it comes to learning about the true days of slavery and where it originated. It holds a background that unleashes the truth about the similarities of how we all live in today's society. Before we chase our dreams, we must not let the influences within our past affect us in the present or future.

The way our people lived in the past will show us what we need to do for us to live in the present, but how we need to prepare for the future. The past lives of our ancestor's sprits connect with ours because we share the same pain as they did, especially as black inner-city children. Black history will not only change your social habits, but you will begin to understand society, other ethnicities, and also your intellectual perceptions.

If you feel that history doesn't matter, and you absolutely have no interest in learning it, then you, my friend, are holding yourself back drastically. We all have made mistakes in our life-time, and some of those mistakes can still be affecting our lives

24

right now just as learning our history can explain a lot of things, we don't understand about the way things are today.

Most young blacks do not really look into history or know about influential black figures who have risked their lives to make this society a better place. Historic individuals such as Malcom x, Martin Luther King Jr., and Rosa Parks should be studied in and outside of school. Usually in black communities and schools, these figures are just talked about, yet it seems no one wants to take the time to dig deeper and truly research what they really accomplished for Black Americans.

In doing so, America could also answer a multitude of questions we all have about this entire case. Throughout the years, our legal history has never played in our favor. However, do not feel as if your life and future are not important; do not think just because you're black that your history is irrelevant. The longer we continue to allow this materialistic society to slowly blind us from reality, the longer it will take us to overcome all the obstacles that we are intimidated by. We are simply wasting time, fascinated with thug life; we continue to negatively socialize on a routine basis, which causes us to get lost in each other's ignorance. Vital information in this country is becoming more classified because some people are aware of our ignorance. They use the awareness of it as a way to disclose the information in exclusive locations.

If we all want to unite with each other as a whole, Americans must take control of their actions and rise up from poverty. The more time we spend wondering and waiting for society to change for us, the longer it will be before we finally discover what it means and how it feels to get it done ourselves. The more independent we are, the more we can focus on ourselves, rather than popular culture.

We, as minorities, need to challenge our intellect in order for us to prove ourselves to that little voice we all have in the back of our heads. Next, if we prove ourselves to the world, we will be better set to plan for the future. The fashion we do this in is not for the racist whites, but for ourselves. We need to show ourselves we can all do something meaningful for society. If we let go of our superficial attitudes, we will surely recognize success is hanging within reach over our heads and all we need to do is look up. We have fear when it comes to learning and we push ourselves away from it.

Out of all the major fears that we currently push our minds away from, don't let the history of your own people be one of them. After all the time we have spent suffering from a diversity of misfortunes, we need to collectively give interest to each other's opinions from an emotional side. If we do so, we can compensate for all the struggling and striving we have encountered over the years. Unless you want to stay at the bottom of every statistical list forever, which I think most of us don't, then we must seize every indication of opportunity that stops in our pathway.

CHAPTER FIVE

Why Was Trayvon Martin His Own Cause of Death?

America has maintained this ignorant habit of judging individuals by their skin color. And, racist white America does not perceive us as African Americans based on the content of our character. Aside from all the cases we see nationally televised, there are factual relations that we conceive of our own when we see injustice globalized right in front of our faces. Due to the circumstances in the Trayvon Martin case, it was all about closure for black teenagers, as well as black adults.

We wanted to verify if this country had moved forward in the legal system, along with the political election of the first black president. If this verdict was manslaughter with at least five or ten years of jail time attached to it, I guarantee you, America, young black teenagers, both males and females, would have gained just enough assurance for us to believe in serving a purpose in this critical American society.

This case did not only indicate racism within the judicial system, but even the investigators showed a lackadaisical attitude when it came to the fundamentals of their jobs. It wasn't just one group of authorities that conducted this haphazard investigation. The police were lazily engaged, considering their offhand interest, and the coroners were not thorough, considering the fact they didn't bag the victim's clothes at the accurate time. We all know Trayvon Martin was black; however, if he was a white male, it's certain they would have closed in on their fundamentals of the investigation and perhaps the jury would have turned out a different resolution.

We took a look inside the jury's debatable opinions and we felt like we could theorize the possibility of what they would consider when compared to the circumstances of the case. We all assumed the jury would review the situation as a young boy walking home from the store, losing his life for no reason other than he was stalked like prey. At least, that's what we felt deep inside and we thought everyone else would see it like that as well. We assumed the jury would review the situation as a young boy walking home from the store losing his life in a horrific circumstance perpetuated by an adult 12 years older than him. The evasive opinions of some non-blacks and white America still linger in their characteristic profile of blacks.

Everyone that took the side on George Zimmerman's behalf displayed a sign of one-sidedness when it came to their explanations contrasted to the evaluations of their argument.

Why couldn't the jury give Trayvon Martin the benefit of the doubt? Why was he viewed as the aggressor, rather than the unarmed teenager? One last query for you, America; why was the jury so quick to negatively malign Trayvon Martin's character as opposed to George Zimmerman's character?

Trayvon Martin was viewed as the aggressor because when racist non-blacks look into our eyes or speculate about our personality, they hold back from thinking with the humanity side of their brain. George Zimmerman received the benefit of the doubt in every part of this process. The fire and ambition we heard on tape displayed a side of George Zimmerman that the legal system was trying to keep hidden under the battlefields the entire time. Non-blacks and some blacks refute our in-put on the case because they are not too fond of us as individuals. We have yet to be given an answer on what's next for our society and they don't realize that is really all we want to know.

The one-sided membrane that is instilled within the heart of these individuals is overwhelmingly frustrating to us and this is why we were aggressively protesting. What exactly triggered that jury to strongly believe Trayvon Martin started that altercation? Although George Zimmerman's minor injuries prove that he was in a fight, they do not prove that he didn't start the altercation.

Starting from the investigation, we thought the judicial system would view the case from the side of public opinion, as they usually do everywhere across America. Once the case reached the court system there was a dramatic shift on the focus and the spotlight immediately closed in on George Zimmerman. It's not the fact that they closed in on him, but the fact everyone came off in a dreamy state in regards to his character, that is what makes us hysterical.

Considering the fact that most of the jury has children of their own, they still seemed as if they could not relate to Trayvon Martin, or his parents, from the legal side of the case nor from the humanity side of the case. Usually when jurors judge a case of this magnitude, they compare and contrast their own personal speculations to the situation, based on the evidence in order to conceive different outlooks on their evaluations. Once the Jurors use this technique to evaluate a conclusion, they use a small amount of their common sense.

Although I am not aware of the jurors' educational backgrounds, I assumed they had capable, logical intellect. However, it seems as though they did not want to use their common sense because they knew it would play a part with their humanitarian side. Because of the fact they turned away from their humanity reveals another reason why black America is so angry behind this verdict.

In addition, you have a juror member that boldly conducted a nationally televised interview on CNN. She expressed the most sympathetic views in favor of George Zimmerman. As juror B-37 went about expressing herself in the interview, she made it clear that her mind was already made up. When she was questioned in the interview on how she felt about the opening statements, specifically to the Don West joke, "Knock Knock, who's there? George Zimmerman. George Zimmerman who? Alright good, you are on the jury. "She replied to Anderson Cooper and said, "The joke was horrible; nobody got it. I didn't get it until later, and then I thought about it and then I'm like I guess it could have been funny, but not in the context he told it."

The tone of voice she replied in came off as engaging to the question. You pick up on the characteristics of her personality when you compare the tone of voice she used when asked more sentimental questions. When she says that she thought about the question later, it was really a slap in the face to all black Americans. Bottom line, a young boy was pursued, shot, and killed.

The juror did not seem to care about that because rather than thinking effortlessly on ways to seek justice, she was thinking of a joke that was meaninglessly, used just to reflect on if it was funny or not. When Anderson Cooper asked juror B-37 why one of the other juror's thought the voice on the tape was Trayvon Martin's she said, the following:

"Well, she didn't think it was Trayvon's. She just said it could have been Trayvon's." Anderson Cooper replies, "So she wasn't even sure?" Juror B-37 says, "No, she wanted to give everybody absolute; out of being guilty."

The major issue in this remark is the fact that she says the other juror wanted to get everybody out of being guilty. Who is everybody? Who was the juror referring to? Certainly not Trayvon Martin because he was killed and considering how many times they looked past him, it would be foolish to suggest. The only person they could possibly be talking about was George Zimmerman. It was clear that most of the people who testified on Trayvon Martin's behalf were not found credible when it came down to their decision.

Why did that juror say she wanted to get everybody off not guilty so soon in the deliberation? It's as if they held our hearts in their hands for sixteen hours, trying to find a way to let the killer of a young black male be set free. In other words, she wanted George Zimmerman to get away with murder.

If you look at her word usage, you can see that her English is very limited. As she struggled to utter her response with fluency, you could pick up on her inability to answer his question with swift elaboration. As she got caught got up trying to answer his question, she made a slight mistake on what she really wanted to imply. After she stumbled across her true answer in her brain, she tried to maintain her composure because she wanted to avoid telling Anderson Cooper what was really discussed behind closed doors in that jury room. Opposed to other questions she was asked she didn't seem so fluent because she had to stop and think of another way to put the real answer in another context.

If we connect the characteristic breakdown with all the other questionable identities that are revealed from the juror's composure, we can then connect it with the fact they didn't want to relate to Trayvon Martin.

Behind her shadow on CNN, we heard her say that she felt the block of cement presented in court by the defense was more compelling, more relevant, than the last two items purchased by a living human being before he was pursued and killed. There's a huge problem with someone dismissing the importance of another human being's last items in their possession.

Any average human being with sentimental logic would defiantly have some kind of recognition of the emotional attachments that play a part with human life. Something must have contributed to the jury's inability to relate to Trayvon Martin or his parents. For someone to automatically infer that this case was not about race than they would almost have to be oblivious to the clarity of what is reality.

It's apparent that Trayvon Martin was a young black male who lived in a high crime environment. He just so happens to be wearing a sweat jacket that is commonly worn by all young teenagers. Just to clarify, there is a stereotype that infers all black males wear hoodies. Considering the weather conditions, he was in the jacket which was a reasonable choice of clothing; therefore, that stereotype can be revoked.

Although we can conclude this from common sense, it questions the logic of George Zimmerman's perception of Trayvon Martin as he was walking home. Considering the speculation that the jury was aware of this, it seemed to demonstrate their inability to relate to Trayvon Martin or his parents.

Repeatedly in this case, the jury easily looked passed Trayvon Martin's rights with no hesitation. Trayvon Martin was walking back to his house and George Zimmerman stepped out of his boundaries due to the fact he informed police that he wasn't familiar with the area where the incident took place. If he knew he wasn't familiar with the area, what gave him the authority to theorize about the people in the area? He did not only deputize himself to the situation, but he also acted on it, as if he was engaging himself in a regular civilized activity.

CHAPTER SIX

As young black individuals, we are curious to everything that happens in our communities, along with the different individuals that we see in associations to our peers. No matter the location, we sometimes feel the need to make confrontational eye contact with people from rival neighborhoods or any unfamiliar faces that may cross our paths. There are times when we assume others are judging us in the back of their minds, and we are only curious as to their purpose or position.

If you play this in part with the ambitious anticipation that George Zimmerman displayed you can understand why Trayvon Martin uttered the words "creepy ass cracker". To white America, this seemingly derogatory statement was not said in contempt for George Zimmerman, but it was said as a simple remark from Trayvon Martin to his friend over the phone.

Possibly viewing George Zimmerman's questionable demeanor as humorous, Trayvon Martin utters the words, "Creepy ass cracker."

Subsequently, the autopsy results revealed that Trayvon Martin had traces of THC in his system. When you are under the influence of marijuana, you see almost everything from your

34

humorous side and you refer to things indirectly or jokingly when you don't realistically mean them. Relating to experience, marijuana can trigger different thoughts, different views, both positive and negative, which causes our intellect to perceive several images that formulate in our head simultaneously.

If the jury made any negative speculation of Trayvon Martin's character, such as his speculated aggressive attitude, then allow me to clarify. If he was under the influence of marijuana at the time, and he was on his way home from the store, he wouldn't have been worried about some white guy, or creepy ass cracker pacing around the neighborhood where his father lived. Considering the fact that he didn't reside at his father's house, he would not have been familiar with everyone in the area.

Black people who live in poverty are seen as beasts or savages by the very few misfortunate non blacks who stay in our communities. Now that we can clarify the jury's sure sense of racism they had in their hearts as they judged this verdict, it raises a few more rhetorical questions for you, America.

What exactly did those jury instructions articulate to their logical intellect, aside from the legal standpoint of the case? Before the trial started, why weren't we given an idea of the possibility that George Zimmerman could be set free, considering the fact they made his action out to be so lawful? In other words George Zimmerman was portrayed as the law abiding citizen during the trial and shortly afterwards, in the hands of the media.

From his observant curiosity, Trayvon Martin could have turned around and asked George Zimmerman, "Why are you following me?"

If we do not have the civil rights to ask this question when we are going about our business in our communities, then whoever holds the reconstruction of the laws in this country should take a second look into revising them. Trayvon Martin could have felt compelled to confront George Zimmerman. Due to the possibility of being under the influence of marijuana, his perceptions of George Zimmerman could have been running wild. As the marijuana imbalanced his perceptions, he could have been questioning as to whether or not he would be bringing endangerment to his family and possibly to himself. We are angry because of all the telling circumstances in the situation that were continuously elapsed by a multitude of individuals who have a higher standard of power over us.

Logic in this case was so overwhelming that everybody and their grandmother would have concluded, "Guilty." The popular broadcasting of the case on national television had a number of individuals who debated, as well as expounded their views on the case. Since we don't have the power or the education that these people have on television, we were captivated by their position and we took heed of everything they said as we waited for the jury's decision. Every time someone argued in defense of Trayvon Martin's civil rights, it seemed as if they steadily switched point of views, and then compared it to a debatable civil right that George Zimmerman upheld against his.

When Trayvon Martin's civil rights were debated, someone was always so quick to refute any remark that someone suggested in respect for Trayvon Martin's rights. Once we listened in on what people said in defense of George Zimmerman's rights, we could pick up on certain vibes that some of the CNN analysts displayed towards the camera. As the analysts in support of George Zimmerman argued their points, they started to ignite a high sense of urgency within their position as they angrily explained themselves in the face of America. When George Zimmerman's rights were discussed by these people, it seemed as if the humanistic side of their character became agitated by the sentimental attachment of what was expressed in respect for the life of a black male. As we tried to put in perspective the passionate opinions of these individuals, it became impossible to digest their thoughts when it came to understanding where they were coming from.

George Zimmerman's humane side continuously appeared in social media, displaying a side of him that does not pertain to the actual reason why he was brought into social media in the first place. Before and after the verdict was read, we were given the idea that we didn't mean anything to society based on the tension between the legal analysts aroused as they effortlessly attempted to convey their opinions.

As we became skeptical of the opinions of the legal analysts, we involuntarily imagined the perpetuated images of slavery when it comes in play with the present authority that racist non-black Americans continue to rub in our face. George Zimmerman's rights had a lot more leniency attached to them when argued in negotiation towards Trayvon Martin's. None of the individuals involved in this case maintained the fiery attitude necessary to alter the perceptions of individuals outside the black community.

If the prosecution displayed a dualistic tone of voice when facing the jury in their closing statements, they would have realized it would have been found more credible to them as their arguments varied. The prosecution mishandled their position because they did not play their legal skills in part by considering the civil rights of the victim in order to sway the jury away from the precious innocence perceived of George Zimmerman.

George Zimmerman made some huge mistakes as an adult and he still received the benefit of the doubt from all the popular spectators. Some groups even raised money on the Internet to help with his defense. George Zimmerman's trial cost the state of Sanford Florida, about 670,364. His defense would have cost taxpayers another one million in legal fees if Mark O' Mara and Don West hadn't taken the case. O'Mara and West needed 500,000 just to take on the case, not including any payments for themselves. America gladly used social media in order to take advantage of our emotional vulnerability because of all the anticipation we showed prior to the trial. When the case became nationally televised, we, as young black males and females, all felt that we could understand Trayvon Martin's character. We were sure that any human being, even someone with a bird's eye point of view, would be able to understand that George Zimmerman was the one who was over all guilty.

Most viewed the case in our own minds as a grown man making well-executed decision's leading up to the circumstances.

George Zimmerman sent off negative energy throughout the entire interaction with Trayvon Martin and everyone with average logic can concede to that conclusion. George Zimmerman's spectators were happy to argue the civil rights of the killer, but when asked about the victim's rights, you can notice the agitation in their tone of voice. It's as if their demeanor came across as irritated every time they were asked about the civil rights of the deceased young black victim.

America came to the conclusion that George Zimmerman's civil rights were more lawful, based on this debatable "stand your ground" law that no one in the country had heard of until after this verdict. Protestors all over the country have spoken loud and clear with their actions. Considering the fact I am not from Florida. I cannot debate their legal procedures, but I can explain the actions of my people even though they are on the complete opposite side of the country. One thing that I can clarify is the reason behind our actions. As another young African American male who could have easily been Trayvon Martin, I am at liberty to infer from what I perceive as to the fact Florida residents felt the same way as I did. Florida citizens experience the same legal constrictions that go on within their communities. Although I may not know these protestors personally, I do feel as if I can relate to them when it comes to their anger based on what I go through here in California. If this stand your ground law was so lawful, why didn't the George Zimmerman spectators refer to it more during deliberation? As we hear these irrelevant qualities about George Zimmerman's character, we are even more heartbroken because of the fact the media continued to victimize the suspect and denounce the victim. Everyone had avoided the clarity behind the rights of Trayvon Martin, in the process of trying to display another side of a killer, a perceived heroic killer of a young black male. America loves to shy away from their humanity side, but when they are confronted on it, they always find a way to slip past it, whether it's through denying or finding a legal solution behind it.

CHAPTER SEVEN

Why didn't they broadcast this other side of George Zimmerman, the predator? They only showed him as a law-abiding, concerned citizen as it negated the opinions of young blacks. It doesn't take a rocket scientist to infer that we, as young Black Americans, are looking for closure. If America has any remorse on how we feel, they would not be broadcasting this other side of a killer, knowing that other young Trayvon Martin's are watching. George Zimmerman was the one who boldly perpetrated all the misfortunes in this entire situation.

August 3, 2011, a resident named Ms. Bertalan, was a victim of a home invasion. George Zimmerman paid her a visit, considering the fact that he was the neighborhood watchman. Ms. Bertalan described the perpetrators as two young black males to George Zimmerman. George Zimmerman and Ms. Bertalan discussed the incident over twenty times. She continuously complained to George Zimmerman about how these black males were not caught. They also discussed how one of the suspects involved lived in the same apartment complex as to where the crime took place. One of the suspects was not arrested until December; however, because the suspect was a minor he was released prior to February 2012. Since George Zimmerman spoke to Ms. Bertalan approximately twenty times, it's highly possible that she informed him of the suspects release date.

Many tried to argue that George Zimmerman would have targeted anyone in that area without regard to race. Considering the fact Trayvon Martin fit the description of the suspects described there is no way he could have looked passed his race.

One the night in question George Zimmerman placed a 911 call reporting a real suspicious guy. The dispatcher on the 911 call asked him was he following the guy. George Zimmerman replied, "Yes." The dispatcher responded and said, "Ok. We don't need you to do that." George Zimmerman chose to follow the victim anyway. George Zimmerman could have prevented the entire situation. Instead of following orders, he did everything in is power to over step his boundaries.

There was a witness who informed police that she heard arguing. If George Zimmerman over stepped his boundaries with police, there is no question he overstepped them with a teenager. Many tried to say the voice on the tape was George Zimmerman's. America, what are the odds of a seventeen-year-old teenager on the phone and under the influence of marijuana putting up a fight against a twenty-nine-year old adult who was sober and had experience in law enforcement training?

CHAPTER EIGHT

In the beginning of this case, the media showed America pictures of both individuals involved. As the investigation moved forward, the media all of a sudden changed the pictures of the killer and the victim because of the perceptions that spectators began to generate. It's as though they were trying to imply something to America as the popularity of the case progressed. It's as if they asked George Zimmerman for a more respectable picture as it got closer to the trial. The pressure from black communities became so overwhelming for them, they had to find a way to shift gear on us.

They asked George Zimmerman for another picture because as time went on they wanted to conceive enough perception through America's social media. They used the popularity of social media to throw off the logic of the vulnerable Americans who use these well conducted websites to escape from reality. As the trial became near, we started to hear more people gradually take the defense of George Zimmerman as time went on. Then we saw the pictures of the black male start to evolve into an image that made him look more violent to some people who didn't want to take the time to understand the black community.

Unfortunately, these ignorant people with misused authority engaged themselves in televised conversations and took the side on behalf of George Zimmerman. They began to instill their own ignorance into other people who were lost spiritually, and then, all of a sudden, it became a battlefield between both sides of the case. Every person who takes the side of George Zimmerman is never really able to breakdown the circumstances to draw reasonable conclusions.

As we watched Ms. Bertalan present her testimony, it leaves black America speculating why she was put on the stand in the first place. It seems that her testimony was used to portray George Zimmerman as the heroic neighborhood watchman. Her experience with the home invasion had nothing to do with the victim who was wrongly profiled. Her testimony shared nothing leading up to the victim's death, but it did serve a purpose when it came to portraying the victim as a criminal. Since she was invaded by two young black males, it seemed to give George Zimmerman the right to kill anyone of that description. The purpose of this testimony seemed to throw off the logic of the jury when it came to making their decision based on the death of this black male.

As the jury focused in on Ms. Bertalan's testimony, I'm sure they subconsciously seconded guessed the victim's moral character when comparing them to the home invasion suspects. If they developed any sorrow for Ms. Bertalan while watching her testify, it surely would have thrown off the logical and legal judgements that the jury had in regards to Trayvon Martin. This was used to sway the jury's opinion to compare Trayvon Martin to the two home invasion suspects. The entire trail seemed to be based on making George Zimmerman look like a hero. Everything was all about making the killer look innocent and making the victim look guilty.

All these non-blacks who testified on the behalf of George Zimmerman were very bad actors. They all seemed so relaxed and sure of something as they engaged in their conversations with the defense. The jury had to sit and watch this lovely performance as the court room allowed this travesty of justice to be conducted, dead in our faces. As some individuals got caught up in the testimony, they looked past the life of the young black male.

George Zimmerman sat at the defense table with a very confident composer. Although his life hung in the battlefield, he never showed any remorse. He took in the revision of his alleged story of his presumed heroic actions. It's as though this helpless white woman ordered a hit on any black male in the community to send a message implying to us we can legally be killed if someone within our ethnical backgrounds does something unlawful to a non-black.

The masterful performance put on by all these people with power caused us to sit back and watch because we are treated by their positions because of where we stand financially and politically.

As Rachel Jeantel took the stand and presented her testimony, she seemed very intimidated by the attorney, Don West. We saw a tremendous shift of arrogance in his character as he noticed her lack of confidence. He started to gain a sudden swagger in his persona as he questioned her. Don West was aware of his intimidating position he had over Rachel Jeantel and he used it to break down her communication skills. He also used this intimidation to throw off the logic of her testimony. He seemed to know how to attack the credibility of Trayvon Martin and got into the head of Rachel Jeantel as he confidently held his composure.

He knew she felt intimidated by his position due to her educational background. He used it to his advantage to throw off the logic of her disposition. Once he was finished, there was an emergence of silence in the court room, which implied reasonable doubt in the perceptions of people who didn't have the logic to recognize the message that was being put into play. However, no one in this case wanted to compare George Zimmerman's murderous actions to his character that was based on the actual criteria leading up to the death of Trayvon Martin. It's as though they spent their entire time searching for a way to acquit George Zimmerman. Although we clearly recognized there were no black people discussing these issues in the court room, we would assume the non-Blacks would be talking about the death of the victim, rather than the life of the perpetrator.

As lawyers from both sides approached the judge, they all conducted themselves as if they were fond of each other. When they looked into each other's eyes, they implied interest in each other's ideas as they discussed their take on the case. Once they stepped into action, their entire composure shifted back into average gear, as they conducted themselves as if they were actually looking into the camera. The whole time all these events came into play, George Zimmerman sat at the defense table with a bored look on his face, as if he and his attorneys had already discussed a way to get him out of this painful circumstance.

As the camera closed in on George Zimmerman, he never showed any signs of emotions as he listened to the details of Trayvon's murder that America proclaims was such a hardship for his delicate character. Even after the verdict was read, he still maintained his arrogant facial expressions that was a sharp contrast to what he was hearing.

After the pronouncement of the verdict, Zimmerman did not express any remorse as he heard the relieving words of "not guilty." After he heard these two words, he glanced at his attorney with a cocky smirk on his face. He gave a slight smile and winked at him in respect for their spectacular performance. If George Zimmerman was so hopeless, why didn't he conduct himself under the same fearful perceptions he'd had when he followed Trayvon Martin? How did these smart people that held more power than us look past all these logical explanations as they conducted themselves in a way that looked so reprehensible to us? As defense Attorney Don West smiled back into the face of George Zimmerman, he possessed a sure, arrogant look. Just the look exchanged between the lawyer and his client, Zimmerman, spoke volumes. It was as if that's what they were waiting for a not guilty verdict the entire time.

Trayvon Martin was his own cause of death because of America's well thought-out plan to use and abuse social media to their advantage. Social media altered the appearance of both the victim and suspect with just a switch of a few photographs. The media used the popularity of television to gradually deceive our opinions because they were aware of our vulnerability. Racist non-blacks and their one-sided opinions have the influence to change the minds of the critics. News analysts abused the ignorance of this country to cast aspersion against Black America for even protesting the verdicts. According to this verdict, Trayvon Martin was his own cause of death because he was a young black male, in the wrong place, at the wrong time with a prejudiced White-Hispanic man.

CHAPTER NINE

Why Should We Consider Becoming More Educated?

As America allows popular culture, social media, and statistics to attack the credibility of our education, we are driven by public opinion. We immediately sink into their knowledge when it comes to things of which we are unsure. We engage in meaningless behavior to run away from the constant ordeals we have to face when we are in reality.

Since the people with power are aware of this communal blindness, they use it to format our logic into something they want us to believe. As the years go on, generation after generation, our families are straddled by this dysfunction. Meantime, we continue to live our lives according to America's racial discrimination system. The more vulnerable we become, the more authority we give them to control our lives. When we show and express our vulnerability, we give them more opportunities to mislead our personal perceptions as they masterfully did in this case.

The increasing population of people of color is currently arising in this country, which brings more vulnerable people to interact with others who are searching for questions. As the differences in our opinions conflict with one another, we can't challenge ourselves to come up with our own answers.

We live on and we continue to be shocked more and more by the ongoing assaults on Black men, in spite of "The Black Lives Matter" movement. We are constantly thrown off with messages in the media. Now they are watering down the message with "Cops Lives Matter." When we are thrown off by the negative ideas that other people put into our heads, we never take the time to focus in on the positive aspects of our lives. As time moves on, we are thrown off by the small things that we hear through social media, and we forget that we are in control of our own destiny.

Once we stop and get past our confusion, we can move past our challenges and take action. But instead, we engage ourselves in even more meaningless activities such as disrespecting one another that serve no purpose as to what we can truly accomplish. As we go on with our lives, it becomes a constant uphill battle between society and the growth of our characters. When we pass up on opportunities, we pass up on time. The more time we spend focusing on the small things, we never take the time to analyze the things that are most important to what we truly stand for.

America's hip hop popularity consists of belligerent lyrics that don't help us become in tune with our true selves. America continuously catches on to what makes us vulnerable, and they keep using it to blind us with the reality of socialism. The ones who are in tune with the white man's game have enough logic to go about their business and move up in society as they watch the rest of us procrastinate.

America loves to throw small obstacles in our face and smile as they hide their true intentions. It is a smoke screen to keep us struggling from one goal to the next. We get more advanced educational degrees, yet we still remain in a paycheck-to-paycheck mode. We still do not own businesses such as Google, Paypal, Facebook, Twitter, Apple, or anything that is making a significant change in technology or that can make the type of money their businesses take for granted. Because we do not own a significant portion of the wealth, even with Black politicians, we do not have economic clout.

Added to this, society has a biased point of view against Black men, which we witnessed when they didn't give a fair assessment in the Trayvon Martin's case.

If you sink into a person's character, you will be able to recognize their intention as they throw their verbal manipulations in your direction. America continues to use their arrogance to challenge and thow off the confidence of vulnerable Americans across the country.

Considering the fact white America used to own us, they are fully aware of our weaknesses and they use their knowledge to put on magnificent shows as they did once again. If they wouldn't have conducted themselves so foolishly in the courtroom during the Trayvon Martin case, they would have recognized what they were truly making themselves out to be—hypocrites.

They were so caught up with their own standards of living, their own financial backgrounds, they really sent off a condescending air that they considered themselves better than us. Since they become so caught up in their misused power, they never paid attention to their humanity. Their character deficits becomes easy to read. As they get caught up in their white privilege, they pass on their ignorance to their children.

When I was a little boy, I would always be curious as to why the white teachers would treat us differently than the white students. As I looked into their eyes with my challenging and humorous expressions, they looked away. They could never look me in the eye.

Although they felt as if they can break down who we are, they have not been able to break down our spiritual core during our four hundred years of being in this land. I became curious as to why they made us feel this way. I started to analyze why. As I held my composure and stayed true to who I was and who I truly wanted be, I learned how to study people. The ability to catch on to what people were articulating through their eyes and body language became very easy to understand. They always use their power to attack our character and as they do so they don't realize how foolish they look while trying to maintain their ignorance. I tried to maintain my masculinity from using my competitive ambition to prove myself to people I think may have doubted me along the way.

I focused on what America portrayed as glamorous and played it in part with what they wanted, which made me fake and not true to my personality. I was tired of being distracted by the constant bombardment of the media. I realized what America tried to force me to believe. I looked into it to just see for myself what their intentions were. I was curious as to what I wanted to know for myself so I could grow logically like everyone else who had more than I did. I started to step into both sides of the constant uphill battle we face amongst each other. As I look at these people who broke my perceptions of things I wanted to know, I reflected on how they made me feel. At first, I analyzed their dreamy living standards and compared them to mine. I focused in on how they conducted themselves and it became clear that the power you hold with your American authority and white privilege do not matter. If you don't compare and contrast who you are and who you really want to be, you become confused with all these meaningless perceptions that further trigger your ignorance.

It's as though we step outside the confinement of our homes and we shift our characters because of the opinions other people may assume. When we say something meaningful to people they develop a weird look on their face, as if we are crazy. As we see these looks, they send a challenging sensation through our hearts and minds, which give us questionable speculation on our dialogue. As we notice the curious looks on people's faces, we are thrilled that someone chooses to take the interest to even listen to us. We take advantage of their attention and, as we try to think, our train of thought gets lost because were not used to having the attention. We get into to something and as we try to explain it, we can't come up with what we thought previously. We stumble across our own words and we can't put into context what we really wanted to say. Our English is thrown off and people look at us as if we don't have the ability to articulate our ideas.

As we engage in more dialogues with different individuals, we stop thinking of meaningful things to say. The small things become so easy to engage in. We keep finding ways to stay in tune with them. Once the major issues come into play, we can't think of a way to act on them so we stop talking about things that could be hard to explain. I try to help some of my peers and family members with what they are trying to say, but when I say one articulate thing, they give me a shocked look in their eyes, as if I was incapable of such a statement.

When it seems no one in your age group wants to engage in meaningful conversations, you seclude yourself away from them because you don't want to give them the wrong impression. We have no choice but to turn to older individuals who can understand our positions when it comes to our ethnicity. People who are in tune with their cultural background give us a slight sense of joy because they see we want to educate ourselves. As we see the understanding on their face, it motivates us more to say what we want to say and we are able to gain confidence as we go on.

The more we see the doubtful looks in people's eyes, the more we realize how ignorant they look. Since they only think with one side of their brains based on this American society, it affects their logic and throws off their humanism. They don't think with their humanity side as they speak; therefore, they don't realize the critical facial expressions they give us. They always use their body language and sarcasm to show what they are truly thinking in their heads. They continuously send of body language that suggests they are better than us because of their living standards. Some of these people come from the same backgrounds we do, since they kept running from their people they are confused on what side they want to stick with. If their logic didn't get thrown off by all the big things in life, they would realize how much enjoyment the small things bring in life.

Once people despise our characters, they despise our full intentions based on their ignorance of our ethnical backgrounds. We never receive any interest from the people we dream of becoming in the future so we become intimidated by their power over us. There is a multitude of genuine people from black communities across the country that have people that are mis-understood by influential people they want to become one day.

I was tired of watching my people be shut down and I wanted to help them build up their self-esteem so I could help them express themselves. I watched my friends develop hurtful looks on their face because all they wanted to do was express what they were feeling. I felt sorry for my peers because all I wanted to do was understand why non-black people always made us feel left out. They wanted to use and abuse their power they had over us because they see the curious looks we have in our eyes when we look at them.

CHAPTER TEN

As a child that never read books, my mother would try to do the best she could to get me to open one. Every time she gave me one, I would set it back down because I didn't feel confident enough to read one. She saw I never challenged myself and one day reminded me of an old myth that whites used to mock blacks. "If you want to hide something from a nigger put it in a book because they won't open it."

This myth made my heart drop to my stomach because it felt like they were laughing in my face. When I thought about the intentions behind this myth, I dropped my head in shame because I was actually making their mocking correlation true.

As all these things killed my character, I never had anyone to turn to for help most times. Even my own mother wasn't around because she was always at work trying to make ends meet. I wondered why I was irritated by white teachers who mistreated us. The look they gave me always provoked an urge in me that wanted to breakdown their character stronger than they broke down mines. This hurtful look of hate on their faces made me feel like I had no control on what I wanted to accomplish in school. It reminded me of something I thought I felt before, but I wasn't all the way sure. As I strengthened my personality I analyzed their hostility towards me and noticed they weren't angry about something I did. I knew I wasn't a bad person so I just watched racist whites as they implied to me that they wanted to perpetuate the continuation of slavery in this evolved society.

Over one hundred and fifty years ago, it was against the law for blacks to read, write, or even observe anything that would help them educationally. If blacks were caught reading, we would be risking our lives to do so. If we engaged in any activities that would logically help us, we would be taking risks at being invariably beaten and perhaps lynched for our curiosity. As inconceivable as this is, it would seem as if we would be more motivated for education in our communities. Due to the negative energy that is provoked in our communities, we are intimidated by the power we think they have over us. We stay within our own environments because we fear the intimidation these people project into our lives. As we pick up on these vibes, we don't want to include ourselves in the ignorance of these racist non-blacks.

We isolate ourselves away from each other. People still don't care to look into the issues of race because they are so in tune with the arrogant side of the oppressor's character. They think the worst of our intentions as they judge us based on our backgrounds and skin color. They see we continue to exclude ourselves from society, and each other, so they use their authority to disturb our environments, such as what we see in the recent rash of police brutality. The harsh mistreatment causes us to feel so threatened by their authority, they keep us from challenging ourselves in other aspects.

They say we all have equal opportunity as everyone else, but due to their systemic discrimination, we don't gain the confidence we need to go about finding opportunities. We live on as if we don't care about the pain our people have suffered from in the past because we don't recognize the anger and frustration they have lived through. We sit back carelessly caught up in America's popular hip hop culture and we don't think back in time to compare our ancestors' past lives to today's life. If our ancestors would have had the equal opportunities we have today, we would realize that we are missing out in life. Our problem is we become distracted by publicity in popular culture. If our forefathers were still alive today, they would constantly fight until the death to expose this corrupted American society.

America didn't want to see us prevail in their presence as they imposed unlawful systems to hold us back from what we could truly accomplish. Once black power movements started, white America was threatened by the progression and uplifted spirits it brought to our communities. They saw the idealization and interest we took in these positive role models, and they didn't want it to continue as we lived on. They hated the positive men such as Martin Luther King and Malcolm X who were trying to uplift the black race. They didn't like how they empowered our nationwide and international community. These men were killed because they were educated black men. Mainstream America wanted us to become musicians, athletes, and entertainers so we will never step into their high-powered world and interact with them on an equal basis.

The white master figured if he could get us to study things that look glamorous to us because of our misfortunes, we will become fascinated with them and only focus in on those particular things. It's as though he knows what we can truly become if we use our natural, God-given brain. Thus, he organizes captivating schemes to distract our state of mind.

America's popular culture continues to throw off our logic as they conduct these meaningless TV shows, including reality shows, and carry on as if it serves a purpose to us. Our obvious misfortunes make us vulnerable as we play into their hands. They take advantage of us and act as if they don't understand. Social media passes down this popular culture along with the stereotypes of the black race to keep their non-black children in position to stay at the top of the list in every statistic. The highest income. The most educated. The most business owners. The most wealthy.

There are millions who aren't in tune with their entire purpose in this world and they live by what America wants them to live by. They argue against people who bring a sense of Afrocentric logic into the discussion and refute what you say with their American logic.

We all know we want to become something big in life, but we don't have the confidence to look into what it is we truly want to be. When we test ourselves, we give up too soon. We don't focus on what our hearts feel so we just say we want to become musicians or athletes to answer their questions. As we continue to answer these questions, we start to believe these are the only things we can do so it becomes the only thing we focus on based on their statistics. They give us so much admiration and glamorous perceptions of the rappers, entertainers and athletes. We look up to these people because we don't even challenge our intellect that we are capable of achieving in the sciences or in the much underrepresented areas of technology.

Several generations are so misfortunate, they lose their gifted characteristics of holding themselves together and focus on statistics and not their real talents. We suffer so much emotional distress, we don't think from the emotional side deep down in our heart. We never explain ourselves from deep down. We only live on the surface. Like robots, we go to unfulfilling jobs, day in and day out, never finding our true passion and purpose.

Since we never focus in on how to get in touch with our true character, we continue to use our aggressive side to express ourselves. We feel embarrassed when we show our emotional sides to each other. We say things in a certain way so no one will laugh at us. As we conduct ourselves based on what other people may think, we only concentrate on acting one way and we never find our inner opportunist.

If the remembrance of our people doesn't reflect on how you feel now, you may not be in tune with your full purpose to this world if you don't compare the past to the future. Having an open mind for education can give us an idea on how to help others. If we want to achieve the things we want, you have to get in touch with your progenitors. The longer it takes us to recognize who we are, the longer it will take for us to figure out what we need to know for ourselves and our future generations. If we stay away from unproductive things, we can apply the proper actions necessary to fight for our humanity. Always remember, education is the key to setting your mind free, and it is also the movement from darkness to light.

CHAPTER ELEVEN

What Perpeturated Stereotypes Still Exist Today?

It is now 2015, one hundred and fifty years after slavery, yet even though it's over, there are things that are still being misinterpreted by people outside the black community. As these stereotypes are broadcasted through social media, they make America believe them as everyday life goes on.

As we watched America put on a spectacular performance to portray Trayvon Martin as violent, there are several other black men who get profiled unlawfully as well. Black males are often stopped for tedious reasons by police, as if there is something so suspicious about them. Their blackness raises eyebrows and makes them guilty to the white man's intellect. They always tell us we were stopped because we fit some description in a report, but the real reason they stop us is because they know we are the powerless ones in this society, and they use their loud tone of voice to intimidate our character. They continue to use their aggressive tone of voice to throw off our equilibrium.

If there is a black person in a nice car, the white man always has to stop them just to make sure the car isn't stolen, and if it not, they get some kind of ticket for something frivolous. The rules seem to direct their probable cause reason to stop black male citizens and once legal interactions come into play, they use some tactic to allude to another law.

One day a friend and I decide to ride our bikes to another city. We stopped for a break in a wide open area and as we were sitting on our bikes, a police car approached a red light at a four-way intersection facing our direction. My friend and I had become so accustomed with being stopped for nothing that we would often try to get out of the sight of police every time we saw them so that we don't give them the opportunity to stop us.

As I was eating a bag of chips, my friend alerted me of their presence as he started to pedal in the opposite direction. Before I was able to tell him to stay put, the police car raced towards him and told him to get off the bike. They just happened to be two white men with badges, guns, and attitudes. At this point, I approached the two officers while still on my bike to ask them, "Why did you stop my friend?"

They responded, "Your friend ran when he saw us and you stayed there." After the first officer's response, the other one said, "If you don't want to join him, then get out of here." As I turned back to proceed in the opposite direction, I had a swift change of mind, which caused me to voluntarily get off my bike and join the search party alongside my friend.

I was fully aware that I wasn't in the possession of anything that would get me handcuffed; I had no problem with being searched. As they were removing everything from my pockets and placing them on the hood of the car, they came across my tablet that I use for my music. Once they pulled it out and carelessly dropped it on the hood of the car, it was as though they looked at each other under the guise of curiosity, you could feel the sudden change in their demeanor. They started to ask questions like, "Where did you get it? When did you get it?" Basically, their questions implied I had stolen it.

Since I did not fit their standardized profile of someone who they could believe was worthy enough to be carrying such a device, I suggested to them that they call my mother on my cell phone to ask her because she was the one whose name this device was in. The officer agreed to my suggestion and when he was on the phone with my mother, he had the audacity to ask my mother while she was at work, "Did you steal this? Where did you get it?" After their concise phone conversation was over, the officer hung up in my mother's face. They then let my friend out the car, handcuffed me, and told me I was being arrested for possession of stolen property. As ironic as this was, earlier that very same day I had just left court for clearing a petty ticket that I had received in a similar circumstance prior to this one.

Because they didn't base their authority on their positions, they compromised the situation to find something wrong because they were guilty of racial profiling. When we were in the car, I could not help but to inform the two officers about my awareness of the unlawful legal procedures that had just taken place along with their overt discrimination.

"I can't wait to see you in court," I stated.

Approximately after a twelve minute ride, we arrived at the police station where the officers contacted all of their resources to receive concrete verification that the device was mine. I spent one hour in a small isolated room. Even though I willingly approached them for the sake of a friend, they still did not believe the tablet was mine and for some reason they went above and beyond to find a reason to imprison me only to come to find out that the tablet wasn't stolen.

Finally, once they confirmed the tablet was mine, they wrote me a ticket for not having a light on my bike, as well as not wearing a helmet. It seemed as if they wanted to find something to hold me for; however, after alarming them repeatedly of their unlawful discriminatory actions, along with expressing my anticipation for their scheduled court appearance with me, they seemed to have backed down. Once this court date came, I awaited their arrival and the two officers didn't even have the integrity to show up. I speculated in my head that I wasn't the only one who was aware of the racial discrimination, but they were one hundred percent aware of it as well.

The profiling by non-blacks and authorities in this country is the main reason why America's prisons are overloaded with blacks and our colleges are limited with enrollment of blacks. If there wasn't any profiling in this country and we were treated like human beings, it wouldn't be as much racial tension going in this country. If we were not judged by our skin color according to the legal system, there would be a fair enough chance that more blacks would have a better chance to do more constructive things with their lives.

The one-sided opinions of Americans have caused non-blacks to conduct their character based on the actual American statistics. These American statistics have thrown off the actual intentions of everything we could truly become. Everything we do is represented by these statistics. Everything we do is judged according to their laws, but yet they always give us these perceptions that we are worthless to them. Individuals who don't make people feel good about themselves as a person can hold that person back from what they want in the future.

When we see this, we turn our heads away in shame because of their negative energy and as we go on, we don't feel like we can do anything for anybody in our lifetime. These people continue to become arrogant as they go on and once they see we are vulnerable to their criticism, they start to take advantage of it. It's this kind of ignorance that does not help our country move on as we all live our lives according to this legal system. When the average person in this country is asked who they feel is the best individual to lead the country, according to statistics, they often reply, "The white person." They say it in a mocking tone of voice, as if it's obvious.

What comes to mind is a white man with a badge, a gun, and an attitude because this is what our country is now based on. We always conceive this specific image because this is what is constantly thrown in our face. These activities become average to us as we go on in our lives.

It just so happens to be the powerful white man who has this power over us that holds back our progress. The white man is the one who gets to run this country along with everything else that is applied to its living standards. His white privilege is based on his position to handle his power, which has been handed down for 6 or more generations. We go through these constant uphill battles with police brutality in this country, yet it's as if the police do not suffer any consequences behind murdering unarmed Black males. We assume that the ones who have higher positions than us are the ones who hold the power. But it's a system set up to keep white supremacy and white privilege as the status quo.

The unconstitutional actions that police engage themselves in, such as the constant beating and harassment of black males, perpetuate the dreadful image of a master and his slave. Until some racist white Americans can get over the fact that we are now free from our historical past, there will be no progress for any ethnicity. It takes unity and open-minded people to even have a chance at making progress. There are additional stereotypes that imply blacks as not being capable to serve anything to this society besides entertainment and athletics.

The reason why that stereotype is so agitating is because of the fact it attacks the credentials of our educational capability. Stereotypes like this have hindered the confidence in some blacks. We can all conclude that confidence plays a huge role in our ability to succeed. Over the years, the continuous ridicule of our self-esteem, along with the discriminatory treatment, there are some of us who start to almost believe that there is no other way to succeed in life, at least from an educational standpoint.

This is one of the reasons why education in our communities is often overlooked. As the years go on, and new generations start to build families, some haven't had the same strive for upward mobility, nor the same traditional values for education that other families have maintained over the years. This may explain the lack of confidence, as well as lack of motivation. As we all know confidence is endured by the ones who surround you. It used to be you saw several generations of educated family members, but now you're seeing the parents have more education than the children.

For that black boy whose father is either dead or in jail, whose parents are on drugs, or mother who works two jobs and goes to school, who is living in an environment most would call "the complete ghetto," confidence is very essential.

In addition to these factors, we also have to deal with being misunderstood by people not wanting to listen to us and not caring to understand us. If more people took the time out of their day to attempt to see what life is like in our shoes, it would really change their perceptions. In the eyes of some whites we are seen as nothing more than satisfaction for their entertainment. They look at us as if we are out-of-control buffoons. Just because there are some of us who maintain a sense of humor amongst ourselves, we are not taken seriously by uptight people or anyone else for that matter. To some of us, the humor we express is nothing but ignorance and nonsense to them. It's a big difference between humor and ignorance. There are some of us that have been through so much that we laugh to keep from crying.

I would like to speak on the behalf of our black women and some of the stereotypes they have encountered over the years, even though I cannot elaborate on personal experiences and ordeals that our black women have suffered from these stereotypes. I can say that just as black men are misunderstood, black women are even more misunderstood. When it comes to the hierarchal format, we are arranged in, the black woman sits at the bottom of the list, following behind the white man, white woman, and black man. Our black women have been repeatedly overlooked, unappreciated, and taken advantage of. They have been maligned by white society with characteristics of being aggressive, masculine, and worthless human beings. They are often called "The Angry Black Woman."

These presumptions have had a tremendous effect on the self-esteem and confidence of black women. Black women have not only been haunted and humiliated by these fallacies, they have also been greatly affected emotionally more so than men because of the fact that they are women.

Black women are vulnerable to criticism from the media and they take information personally into their mind and from their hearts. As black women try to connect with black men, they want us to not only listen to them verbally, but they want a man that listen to their hearts. Compared to a man, a woman deals with their need to articulate her feelings. Women often can't find the proper man to express themselves to or anyone else for that matter. The pain that black women go through in this country can affect how they express themselves within society.

As they go on, they lack the confidence to form new relationships with black males, and they eventually lose confidence in their dating capabilities. This emotional distress takes a tremendous toll on the way they conduct themselves. As they continue to try and get through their confusion, they are not able to express themselves to a person, gender or ethnicity. They encounter the continuation of these stereotypes from white society, racist non blacks, and they also receive them from black males in their communities.

There are certain black males that dishearten the characters of black women just as white males have done over the years. Black men disrespect black women and mistreat them because males can be generally blind to the feelings of a woman. The constant mistreatment black women receive causes them to mistrust black men. When women feel this way, they can feel secluded from the world and they will never find a way to express their softer, feminine side. The long term effects these stereotypes have had on Black women is unimaginable. They never meet a male that shows his emotional side so they are scared to show it to them because they don't want to be embarrassed or makes things awkward.

Black women are now looked at in this country as the least capable individuals in the nation. We continue to run from these feelings because the continuation of these perpetuated stereotypes. Black men never stop to review their emotional side and they cause black women not to come in contact with it either. Since black men don't get in touch with who they are, they never think of a way to show their inner feelings. Women notice the expressions on black men's face as they try to engage in emotional discussions and they become slightly intimidated. As they continue to carry themselves, they develop negative attitudes and they reflect on their previous feelings and they continue to carry themselves with the aggressive side of their personality. As our women go on, they never feel they could express themselves to anyone and they show anger towards black men because they see they don't want to express their emotions.

If black men got more in touch with themselves, they would see what a Black women's intentions are as they go along. If we care anything about our own progression as men, we would realize that we don't see it for ourselves. If we could understand Black women's emotional side, we would be able to express our own emotions. As they carry on, they continue to express their aggressive side to us and they try to act accordingly to our destructive behavior. If black men took a look at who they were, they would be able to show their women the care they need to go on. If black men focused on a woman's emotional side and not her privileged bodily functions, then both genders would be able to maintain healthy stabile Black families. If we all took time to focus in on ourselves, we could connect amongst both genders. This is borne out by the statistical fact a higher percentage of black women are single, divorced, or have never been married in America.

If black men reflect on what has happened to black women since slavery, they should have more empathy for their situation.

Black women have gone through more than many races of women, yet they have made some of the greatest strides in history. In the past, Black women were not only beaten or lynched along with their men, they were also raped in front of their spouses.

Once black men try to imagine the long-term emotional distress directed towards black women today, it can explain the bottled-up frustration passed on from previous generations. If black men can come to realize women's emotional needs to feel protected from a general standpoint, they can understand the reasons why women react differently to certain situations.

The stereotypes of black women being masculine are insane. Black women have had to carry the weight of a man when their men have been absent, but they are still feminine.

However, it is a well-known fact that black women are as mentally tough as anyone of any race or gender. Black women are flourishing when it comes to holding a family together, as well as keeping themselves emotionally controlled for the sake of their children's well-being. Not only do they keep their children strong and keep themselves strong, but they continue to manage all these hefty situations. Along with the seemingly impossible task of financing a single parent household, they have done it for years independently, and they do it for their children.

Unappreciated qualities like these that do not receive enough admiration needed for our women bring on what some see as a harshness in Black women. It is difficult to express themselves in more sentimental ways when they are carrying the weight of the world on their shoulders. If they had less responsibility, they would come off as nicer and that would definitely change the perceptions of males. This would happen if more Black men stepped up to the plate and handled their headship in the family, than letting the Black women carry all the weight.

Unfortunately, Black males are oblivious to Black women's feelings. There has become a social divide and rift between the sexes. As a result, they don't know how to go about expressing themselves to each other. Black men do not carry the composure that is necessary to conduct themselves as the gentlemen most Black women want.

Black men do not think of black women as delicate or in need of protection because they have always come off as so strong. They often feel Black women emasculate them because of their strength. But historically, black men and women used to work together in an egalitarian type relationship. The Black women always worked outside the home to help make ends meet.

However, in the recent years, Black men engage themselves in relationships with white women because they think white women are more delicate based on America's mainstream media.

As our black women start to witness black men in these interracial relationships, it shuts down a side of their self-esteem as they move along with their lives. As they see these public relationships, it continues to mock their well-being and undermine the black women's contributions to this country. From all the constant criticism that Black women receive from everyone, they feel as if every male of any race thinks of them in this way.

In conclusion on the subject, I would like to remind black and white America of a nationally known factor on the behalf of black women. Behind every success story, there is a strong black woman that has kept her family on the right path to make that success possible. We all know more times than not, there isn't any success without a black woman. If we, as men, take it upon ourselves to wake up and really smell the coffee, everything else will become ordinary common sense, which will give us the proper push we need to consider the term "ladies first." In other words, we must make our women feel delightfully satisfied with their inner self, so we can feel at least decent for our inner self. Then perhaps we could heal the breach in the relationship between Black men and women.

CHAPTER TWELVE

*What Can We Do Within Our Communities To
Rise Above Poverty?*

There is a multitude of things that we can do to rehabilitate our communities. The fact that we don't respect the space or the property of other individuals only shows that we don't respect ourselves. For example, we throw trash on the ground as if we don't care about the cleanliness our living environments. These careless habits that destroy our communities are unhealthy for our mental development that plays a part with the development of our intellect. All the mixed emotions children feel behind this distress cause them to have problems with the other orientations that bring out who they are. We also have to deal with the poverty of our living environments along with this constant filth we live in.

A major issue that we need to focus on is the fact that we can't get along with each other. Once we come to realize that we are all in the same predicament, we can start to understand each other better. There are too many of us that have such hatred for one another, we have different gangs who will kill each other over turf or the colors we wear or even the destructive sale of drugs. These behaviors are done on property that is controlled by the white man, and possibly owned by him as well.

If we start to recognize that if we don't make a change amongst ourselves, as well as the way we socialize and communicate with each other, we will continue to constrain ourselves from the necessary changes needed for us to socially evolve.

We have detrimental habits ingrained in our communities, such as fighting each other for the most mediocre reasons. Small petty issues that lead to fights often turn into long term violence, which brings us to this intense hatred for one another. Intense hatred causes us to severely harm each other or kill each other. When we act on our mixed emotions and engage in these petty murder schemes, we feel so much violent anger that we only think with the aggressive side of ourselves. This aggressive side that comes with gang membership that most of us will risk dying for, becomes so counterproductive to the reality of what we really want for ourselves. We can't see what we are truly doing to ourselves and to each other.

As ongoing violence continues, these negative influences have a tremendous impact on the mindset of the black youth. These negative influences confuse us as we seem to care less that we are eliminating black males who face the same discrimination that we all do. As black males take it upon themselves to engage themselves to go out and kill another black male, they don't realize that they are only weakening the strength and progression amongst black families. As time continues, society uses our violence as a reason for racial profiling.

No matter what the circumstances are, we continue to pass down the perpetuation of slavery right in front of their faces. Like the Willie Lynch Syndrome, we are pitted against each other through skin color, gang affiliation, or any other division. Young Black men are so angry behind the situation they don't realize they are only killing themselves. As we continue to engage ourselves in these situations, we don't recognize the trauma we suffer behind them. We don't notice we are taking the lives of ourselves and our future when we engage in these activities.

As we continue to involve ourselves in these situations, we forget the long-term trauma it can have on our lifestyles and our family's lifestyles. Once the destruction within the communities continue to erupt, most of which is never heard of through the media. The cries in black communities are very often bypassed by non-blacks in the TV media and in social media. As blacks unified in most areas to protest for Trayvon Martin, racial tension is still very much alive. The racist non-blacks in society mock and laugh at the way we struggle and live in our environments. These issues cause more segregation and much more division within the society. America's prolonged racism affects the way individuals react towards any race. However, most are judged based on personal experiences that may have happened within their lifetime.

If we can all stand up and protest for Trayvon Martin, we should be able to relate to each other. All the George Zimmermans in the world don't even have to get their hands involved with our activities because they see some of us hate ourselves.

These issues cause us to become divided from each other and they force our characters to feel alienated from one another. As we all try to go on in this country, we don't notice America's psychological warfare is causing us to pull each other apart as we try to stay in touch with ourselves.

If we could work on improving these flaws within our community, other people outside our communities won't be able to destroy our communities as well. Even though we are all unique individuals that come from different areas we can all relate to each other when it comes to certain experiences.

We all know what it's like to struggle, to go days without eating and see our mothers wiping tears because they are low on bills. The list of substantial hardships that we all commonly experience can go on and on. If we pause and think about the affect this has on us individually, we start to understand the affects it may have on our peers and everyone else in our community. Once we can collectively identify our similarities, we can begin to collaborate on them and have more unity in our communities. Until these things happen, we will have a long hard way to go.

A major dysfunction we need to address is the repeated use of the most derogatory racial slur known to America such as the N word. There is this conclusive illusion that we have evolved the meaning of the word into defining males in general. We have also changed the spelling to "nigga" instead of the original origin of its spelling. No matter what we assume it means, or what we say it means, it will always hold the same meaning. As it still stands in the dictionary, it has the same meaning. As it still stands in the brain of racist non-blacks, it has the same meaning. As it is almost uttered by racist non-blacks, it has the same meaning, and as it is articulated with anger and anticipation by racist non-blacks it has the same meaning.

Besides the alterations we have made in the words spelling and meaning, why do we feel as if it's so natural to still use? For those of you who do not understand the historical painful intent of the word, allow me to elaborate on its disturbing context. The word "nigga" or "nigger," however you want to spell it, is and was a proudly used derogatory term by the white slave master to drastically mock, hurt, and breakdown the self-esteem of blacks. There are some confused human beings inside and outside of the black community who assume the definition of the N word means black people in general. Anyone with those presumptions should have more expansion in their minds about things of which they are uncertain. This confusion has also played a part in the word being used beyond its means. The exact definition of the word nigger means ignorant. Ignorant means lack of knowledge. If you think about it ,anyone can be called a nigger. It is a term used with the context lack of knowledge, but with the intended content of racism towards uneducated blacks. This can then explain the use of the word directed specifically towards black people, due to the fact that it was against the law for us to gain an education.

White men on a daily basis impulsively took advantage of the N word to arrogantly boast and brag about the superior authority they had over blacks. It was also used to mock, and make fun of black's inability to act on their hostility because of the lawful consequences of being beat to death or hung from a tree and possibly being burned alive while having a rope tied around their necks. As black people, please take the time to try and reflect on that feeling you get when you think about it and then think about how our people felt when they lived it.

Once these ordeals became nothing more than the way of life for blacks, they would start to experience the haunting return of the N word from their own people. In these days the N word was not used as a sign of endearment as it is today; however, it was used by us to offend each other when there was a dispute or disagreement. These disputes and disagreements would go on in the presence of the white man, and often, it was seen as entertainment to him. The continuation of the N word uttered from one black person to another had a specific motive behind it, such as causing another black person to reminisce on the worst times of their lives. This word was also used to verbally express the same devious intent that white men used it in, as well as sustain the same social order that went along with it.

If you can speculate on the emotional intensity of the horrific unforgettable experiences and situations that our people went through, you can understand why the word nigger or nigga is so problematic and unethical in our communities. For us to call and refer to each other as this word is very unnatural.

During the years of slavery, there was frequent animosity between blacks because of the separation of dark skin and light skin. The dark skinned slaves were the ones who worked outside in which they were titled as "field slaves," as for light skinned slaves who were titled as "in house slaves," their duty was to serve and obey the master indoors. The field slave's mandatory duties consisted of picking cotton all hours of the day that would add up to 300-800 pounds a day. In house slaves had mandatory duties such as preparing and serving dinner for the master, as well as cleaning and maintaining the house. The intended purpose of the white man's distinctive scheme to separate us by skin color was to creatively instigate intense disputes between blacks so they could not gain any unity, power, or ideas that would cause us to become a threat to his well-being.

Due to the white man's elaborate scheme to cause dysfunctions in our community, it can explain the reason why blacks uttered the N word towards each other out of anger. As time progressed, the word started to be used jokingly, which evolved the use of the word into being used socially. If the people who were beaten, raped, and lynched heard the excessive way we use the N word today they would be tossing and turning in their graves as of right now. If you evaluate all the historical complexity of the word's intent, you can see why the use of the word needs to be stopped.

Another issue we need to intercept is women being referred to as bitches. This problem has affected the way in which black women perceive themselves. Similar to the N word, this is another term that has been repeatedly used so often that it has now become natural for both black men and black women to say.

Even though we are all aware of the definition of the word, we still surpass the pernicious intent behind it. Black men have used this word so often towards black women that it has caused them to voluntarily refer to themselves as a bitch. This used to have a pejorative or derogatory meaning.

Black men do not only use this word to disrespect black women, but they also use it to describe black women and that is very vulgar. Black men should look at black women with more positive expectations, rather than viewing all of them as bitches or whores. In doing so, we will be perpetuating the same mocking verbal abuse that white men have directed towards black women time and time again throughout history.

Now a days, since it seems as if some women embrace the term, it only makes black men more openly comfortable with using the word more excessively. For us as black men to allow our women to even conceive this idea that they are bitches, we should feel ashamed of our lack of effort and interest in trying to review things from their perspective. You would think that since black women in our communities are extremely vital to us as males, considering the fact they are the ones who gave us life and inspire us to live life, as well as generate rebirth within our community, we would respect them more.

Although some black males are fully aware of the pernicious context of the word's origin, it is so regularly used that it seems almost impossible for them to avoid saying it. In comparison with the use of the "N" word, we can see that we still have major issues on becoming unified as a whole just as we did when we were in the hands of the master. Once you take all this into consideration, you can surely come to think that the racist white man himself is somewhere laughing it up because he doesn't even have to fix his mouth to say these derogatory terms anymore. We are now as of today doing it to ourselves.

Black women, if a man cannot refrain himself from uttering this word towards your well-being or self-esteem, then that man doesn't respect you or understand you as a human being, nor does he respect himself.

The most crucial dilemma that we constantly face in our communities is growing up without fathers. Male figures are essential to have in our families for young black males and black females. Black men have constantly passed on traditions that give their child the wrong ideas on how to hold themselves together as they go on. They become a number to the system just as they were back during slavery. According to the statistics, black men are often killed by another black male. Black men are often so caught up in their own minds, they don't realize what kind of signal they were passing down. All the unrevealed point of views that fatherless children go through do not receive a second opinion on how to conduct themselves as men.

This problem is even more significantly damaging to women because they never have the understanding approach to express themselves. They miss out on the male figure's perspective they need to engage in meaningful conversations. Young women take in these missed communications from growing up fatherless, and are just as negatively affected as male children. They too wind up having a difficult time trying to express themselves so they can show their true intentions behind what they say. These situations always cause our women to run away from their emotional sides as they always feel uncared for, as well as emotionally confused on what they want to do. As they grow older, they continue to lose self-respect for themselves as they tap into what society says they are such as "strippers," bad bitches," and "hootchie mamas," according to these American images.

Black women feel alienated by their fathers and they never have the proper ways to think of emotional ways to express themselves. Black women often trap themselves inside this American dysfunction by looking into white males more than black males. America portrays black males as out-of-control buffoons to keep attacking the logical explanations that come along with it. If black men took the time to analyze the characters of black women, they would be able to conduct themselves based on their comparisons.

Black males who grow up without fathers are more than likely to grow up with lots of hostility. Although some of us are fortunate enough to have strong mothers, we still don't have the male figure necessary to guide us in the right direction. Our mother's help us get in touch with our emotional sides, but we never have the male voice we need to hear in order to receive the proper instruction for the development of our male characters. The lack of a role model of a male figure causes us to constantly search for male role models around our communities.

The corruption of American popular culture destroys the intellectual and spiritual value that black males and women search for. If America can understand why we look past our parents' teachings, they would be able to understand our true intentions when we find negative ways to express ourselves. The uncertainty of young black people cause us to engage in more meaningless activities that throw us off from who really are deep inside. These misunderstood assumptions on the part of blacks have played in part with the way we dress, talk and the way we interact with others.

It's the obligation of the father to give the son the proper way to conduct his behavior based on the way others may treat them. The fundamentals of becoming a gentleman are often never learned because of the negative environmental influence in black communities. If black males do not have this male figure, they try to go along with their mother's standards, but it can do nothing but cause significant damage to their masculine capabilities. As black males seek the male presence on how they need to conduct their behavior, it starts to seem as if we never find the proper role models to tell us how to go about it.

As we try to control our frustration, we end up taking it out on each other, which only makes the suffering worst. We use this anger to by fighting and killing each other. In some neighborhoods, the only influential people we come in contact with are gang members, however, these individuals are sometimes seemingly desirable influences. After a certain amount of time, the opportunity to join a gang becomes very easy and extremely hard to stay away from.

After we start to analyze the formation of this country, we see the mocking perceptions of our peers thrown at us. After a certain amount of time the opportunity to join a gang becomes very easy to engage in. We join into these activities because of the sense of slight encouragement it brings to our characters. We become mocked by the criticism we feel from these people we engage because we don't have any other assurance to show us a different way to behave.

Black fathers that want to actually raise and grow old with their children understand positive parenting can be indispensable factors of life for young black males, as well as for young black women. In contrast, the fathers who are oblivious to their children, as well as heartless towards anyone else's feelings, are truly hurting our communities' progress. These men who fathered children and didn't take care of them don't realize it because some don't have the intellectual capacity to do so. These men do not respect nor understand themselves or the people around them; therefore, sometimes the consequences and effects of their wrongful doings are not clear to their own reflection. Even though they are technically grown men, they are still trapped in the mind of a young confused, misunderstood boy, and because of this, they have never received any validation on what it is to be a man or what it takes to raise a man.

Most importantly, we still have a disproportionate number of fathers that are out there who still don't want to rise up to the occasion of raising his child, be it his son or daughter. These men are not out of their child's life because they are in jail or dead. This specific type of black man is out of his child's life by choice. Also because he has no idea or speculation on what the qualities of being a man or a father are all about, he continues to be a sperm donor and make babies he has no intent on helping to rear. Recently, there was a show on Oprah with men who had fathered as many as 30 plus children. There is no way, as a Black man, you can afford that many children or spend any quality of time with them.

For example, this kind of man shows up every once in a while to visit his child, or possibly just shows up for something that has to do with the mother and his child just happens to be there. No matter how many young black children cherish the very little time they spend with this man, he will never technically qualify or be considered neither as a father nor as a man, for that matter. Black men who fit these descriptions and standards often grow old never considering the well-being of their child. They also have no idea what is to be a traditional man, a black man, a husband, a father, or any other title that may apply. These men not only disown their offspring, but they also have no concern for their grandchildren either. Many of them never saw an example of a father or husband in the home, and they repeat the cycle.

For example, if a young black woman has a father that is incarcerated or dead how is she supposed to learn how to respect men as well as herself as she goes on in this racist and sometimes sexist society? In this kind of situation, young women end up dating these men who treat them like objects, rather than human beings.

For example, if a young black male with a mother that works two jobs and goes to school has a father that is incarcerated or dead along with an unknown grandfather, where is he supposed to turn for that male figure's perspective? In this situation, these young black males usually end up very confused and corrupted by this society, and it also makes them more of a target, considering the fact that they are black males in America.

That is why it is important for us as Black Americans to break the generational curse and break this cycle of fatherlessness.

CONCLUSION

Who Am I? What Inspired Me?

My name is Terrence McCrea. I am twenty-one years old. I am a black male from California and I reside in a low-income housing area in the county of Los Angeles. I was raised by a hard-working, passionate mother who maintained a single parent household, while going to school, also holding down two jobs to support me and my sister who is nine years older than me. My father has been incarcerated for murder since I was four years old; coincidently, the victim was another black male. When I was twelve years old, I lost a brother to gang violence. I have been kicked out of almost every school that I have attended up until I was fourteen years old. Even though I was kicked out during my junior year of high school, I did graduate with my class and walked the stage. I was motivated to finish high school, and my mother was a strong cheerleader. Growing up with no one to turn to when my father was gone and my mother was always at work, it was hard to cope with various situations. Without a doubt, I witnessed and experienced the same obstacles that the majority of black males face.

I myself have had fear in my academic capabilities, and I still do; however, I have viewed my academic fears as just fears and I take those fears, face them, and dismantle them with the best of my ability. Everyone in this world has potential, but it's the action and responsibility that take your potential to the most maximum level of success possible. Just like they say, a mind is a terrible thing to waste. I told myself in a dream that before I left the face of the earth, I wanted to write a book. I did not plan this ahead of time and I didn't think I was prepared to do so at this age; the idea came out of nowhere.

After all the historical cases remembered by black communities, such as the Rodney King case, OJ Simpson case, as well as your own encounters and run ins with the law and racist non-blacks, I felt a need to tell how we, as Blacks, are affected by these landmark cases. Once you witness a high profile case in which the victim is in your age group, the anger, frustration, and emotion really hit home.

Since I am just another Trayvon Martin to society, I felt like I didn't have the credentials to have my point heard on CNN or anywhere else for that matter. I wanted someone to hear what I have to say about this now. I didn't want to wait until I was older. It may be too late by then.

I do not have the power to speak on television; I do not have the power to fly across the country to Florida in order to convey my opinion or even be heard by anyone with higher means in society than me.

I wanted to find a way to talk to the most racist non-blacks in America, as well as the blacks who didn't support Trayvon

Martin in America. I wanted all of the Trayvon Martin's to have a voice so that the racist non-blacks out there can have no choice but to understand where we are coming from and explain to them why we are the way we are as well as breakdown the reasons why we have every right to be angry by this verdict.

To My Peers:

This book was meant for every black male who has been profiled and killed in this American society. Black males who have lost their self-consciousness due to this profiling should not have to suffer behind the continuous prejudice made by the ignorant citizens in today's generation.

Aside from this case, there were a number of other things I wanted my peers to be aware of and the reason why this case touched our hearts so much. If you were to hang out with me for any length of time you would see I am no different from you. In other words I don't speak the way I write when I am with peers. I am also a very passionate person when it comes to my black people that are proud of being black as we all should be. If you have that one wild dream that you laugh at because you think it's undoable or unbelievable, this is living proof that you can do anything you put your mind to. I honestly had no idea I had so much to say. If you have never read a book from start to finish, I hope this one is the first one you have completed. Although I am not a fan of reading myself, I recommend supporting black authors as well. If you don't know of any, here are a few you should look into; Malcolm X, Michael Eric Dyson, Richard

Wright, James Baldwin, and Walter Dean Myers. It is all right to support music artist and athletes in our community, but reading breeds leaders.

The very few people I can thank behind this accomplishment would be my mother because of her hard working and never giving up mentality. I also have been impressed with the inspirational virtue she carries about herself that most mothers don't. The last person I would really like to thank is a very powerful, motivational black studies professor that goes by the name Julie Trager. If I never met Julie Trager at a local community college, I would have never been able to have the determination to get these points expressed. After my very first semester in college, this one professor impacted my life and helped with the shaping of the first and second draft of this book.

In conclusion, if there is a non-black or black person that feels I did not effectively expound on these points, please peacefully use your warfare to get in contact with me and I will gladly debate and discuss with you.

In all peace to President Obama, as another Trayvon Martin, I peacefully ask you for two first class plane tickets so we can further discuss this situation. As a lawyer from Harvard, I have admiration for your standard of education and, as a future defense attorney, I would like to peacefully challenge your position. I have become agitated by the arrogant statistics America continues to conduct regarding Black life. When they throw these statistics right in our face, as if they don't know what we go through, it is very frustrating. Through the spiritual guidance of Martin Luther King, Jr., and Malcolm X, we once again come into peace as we ask you to once again free us from this racist American society.

Lastly, a significant thanks to my ghetto heroes, Bone Thugs N Harmony, who gave me all the right ideas on how to control my anger and frustration as a black male in this corrupted society. I hope for nothing but the best for you all.

CPSIA information can be obtained
at www.ICGtesting.com
Printed in the USA
FSHW011812150521

9 780692 581957